"Barbara Kerkhoff blends her pastoral education, her real-parish experience, and skillful use of professional tools in this book. With these gifts she provides a reflection and guidance source for people serving God and parish community. This resource both fosters pastoral sensitivity and deepens personal spiritual growth. Her synthesis of the INSPIRE project benefits the individual ministry, parish life, and the Church as a whole."

— Rev. Louis Anderson
Grand Rapids, Michigan

"The exploration of the stages of transition provide an invaluable tool that enables personal and pastoral growth. The individual and group reflection questions are exceptional, providing moments for spiritual and human insights to emerge and provoke transformation. Strategies for Effective Transition offer wise, realistic and practical ideas for engaging a pastor transition for parishes of all sizes and circumstance."

— Emily Filippi
Director for Christian Formation
Office of Catholic Education
Diocese of Richmond

Navigating Pastoral Transitions

A Staff Guide

Barbara Kerkhoff

LITURGICAL PRESS
Collegeville, Minnesota

www.litpress.org

Cover design by Stefan Killen Design. Cover photo © Thinkstock.

Library of Congress Cataloging-in-Publication Data

Kerkhoff, Barbara.
    Navigating pastoral transitions : a staff guide / Barbara Kerkhoff.
      pages cm
    Includes bibliographical references.
     ISBN 978-0-8146-3807-1 — ISBN 978-0-8146-3832-3 (ebook)
    1. Catholic Church—Clergy—Relocation—Study and teaching.   I. Title.
  BX1912.K47   2013
  254'.02—dc23

                                                  2013019770

Contents

Preface

The Archdiocese of Chicago and Loyola University Chicago funded this guide through a grant from the Lilly Endowment, Inc. *Sustaining Pastoral Excellence* (SPE) program. Dedicated to finding and sustaining excellent pastoral work in several U.S. Christian denominations, SPE helped the Archdiocese and University found INSPIRE. The INSPIRE project promotes pastoral excellence in parishes of the Archdiocese. Its acronym summarizes its mission: to Identify, Nurture, and Sustain Pastoral Imagination through Resources for Excellence. Serving parish staffs throughout the Archdiocese, INSPIRE helps them develop collaborative expressions of excellence in pastoral leadership.

On behalf of the Archdiocese of Chicago Department of Personnel Services, the Office for Lay Ecclesial Ministry submitted a proposal to INSPIRE recommending a Pastor Transition Study Team to explore the challenges and opportunities inherent in pastor transitions. The task force formed the following question to express their singular mandate: Can we find better ways for priests to make their way to new parishes as pastors?

Subsequently the quest was extended to see how parish staff and parishioner leaders can best work through this difficult time in the life of the parish, and booklets were developed for these groups.

Members of the Study Team designed and implemented surveys of pastors, parish staffs, and parishioner leaders in the Archdiocese of Chicago who had recently experienced a pastor change. The team is grateful for the participation of ordained and lay leaders who generously contributed their observations and insights.

The following persons contributed time and effort to the Archdiocese of Chicago Pastor Transitions Study Team:

Mark Bersano, Assistant Director, INSPIRE
Ralph Bonaccorsi, Office of Conciliation
Rev. James Donovan, Secretary, Priest Placement Board
Rev. Vincent Costello, Co-Vicar for Priests
Daniel Gast, Director, INSPIRE
Rita Kattner, DMin, Office for Councils,
    Christ Renews His Parish
Kathleen Leggdas, Director, Office of Ministerial Evaluation
Carol Walters, Director, Lay Ecclesial Ministry
Cathy Walz, Office for Catechesis and Youth Ministry

Commissioned Author:
Barbara Kerkhoff, MDiv

Barbara Kerkhoff served as one of the INSPIRE project's original Parish Consultants who helped pastoral staffs—pastors, ordained ministers, commissioned lay ecclesial ministers, lay leaders, and staff persons—develop collaborative expressions of pastoral leadership and ministerial practice.

The author acknowledges for their support and insights:

Phyllis DiFuccia, SSJ, INSPIRE Parish Consultant; St. Joseph Academy Vice President of Mission
Dominic Perri, INSPIRE Parish Consultant; Principal at Essential Conversations Group
Participants in a survey of pastoral lay ecclesial ministers and staff persons conducted in the Archdiocese of Chicago, in 2011–2012, with special thanks to participants in three focus groups conducted in August of that year.

Introduction

The pastor is leaving the parish where you serve on staff. What does this mean for the parish? What does this mean for you? What will happen to the programs that parish staff and leaders have worked to create? How can you have any impact on what is happening?

When word of the pastor's leaving gets to the staff, life and ministry are never quite the same. During a time of transition you live and work in a space that holds both questions for the

> "I believe that this is one of the important and positive results of the Council: the co-responsibility of the entire parish, for the parish priest is no longer the only one to animate everything."
> *Pope Benedict XVI*[1]

future and emotions that range from simple anticipation to grief to hopefulness. Sometimes those feelings are all mixed together. You may experience moments of not thinking clearly or low energy. You may pick up conflicting signals from your colleagues, from the pastor who is leaving, and from parishioners who fill in lack of information with assumptions and rumors.

While transitions are normal life experiences, and individually we can describe how we personally navigated a transition in the past, a change of pastors is unique. It is an ecclesial experience. Whether you are paid or unpaid staff, you have a special place and role in the community during a time of pastor transition. Whatever your particular role, a pastor change calls you to new opportunities of service in your ministry. The parish staff can provide stability and familiarity as the parish moves

1

into a time of adjustment and uncertainty. However, here's the irony and here is the question addressed in this guide: "Who ministers to the minister?" The first answer but not the last, you will learn, is *you*. Know that you will not walk this path alone.

In this guide, leaders and parish ministers from the Archdiocese of Chicago will share what many of them learned about serving in a time of pastor transition. The following pages identify dynamics that may occur during a pastor transition, offering resources that support parish staff, both in their ministries to the parish and individually as professional persons. The guide is intended for everyone on parish staff regardless of title. Questions that encourage individual reflection and communal conversation appear at the end of each section. They invite vitally important conversations among three critical partners: staff, parishioner leaders, and pastors.

The Pastoral Leader's Journey

It seems part of our nature to view episodes of change and transition as necessary speed bumps to get over so that we can settle back into "normal" living. With each new change experience, we learn to efficiently perform the necessary tasks that serve a transition: informing others that a change is imminent; setting timelines for projects; rearranging living and working spaces; setting up new procedures. Yet, tasks are only one element of transition. They are important as symbolic markers on the journey, but below the surface lies even more important work. There is the matter of coming to terms with intangible realities, readjusting personal hopes, objectives, and priorities, and coping with challenges to one's spirit and sense of well-being.

Saying good-bye to a departing pastor and welcoming an arriving pastor is both a public event for the community and a private experience for each staff person. In the eyes of the parish community you are a parish leader. Parishioners watch you for clues and cues. It can be helpful to recognize, especially during a pastor transition, that you need to have the grace to be yourself. That grace usually requires seeking the counsel of wise ones who have already traveled this road.

The *Navigating Pastoral Transitions* series comprises three guides addressed to parishioner leaders, to staff persons, and to transitioning pastors themselves. These supplemental resources are not intended to replace the policies and procedures of your own diocese or archdiocese. Links to many such documents are provided at www.litpress.org/pastoraltransitions/resources.

Each text in the series assumes God's active, loving, and transforming presence in all of life's transitions. It also assumes that our partnership with God and God's people leads to life-giving choices that help ensure successful transitions in any situation, particularly ministerial settings.

As you reflect on these materials and dialogue with respected and trusted individuals (colleagues, spiritual director, friend), you may begin to recognize this critical time

> For where two or three are gathered together in my name, there am I in the midst of them.   *(Matt 18:20)*

as an opportunity for renewed engagement in life and a renewed vision of your ministry. This particular transition could easily tempt you to narrow your focus to the "logistics of change," the doing of tasks to just get through it. What a loss of opportunity that would be! It could, however, move you to recognize that change can be transformative. It will involve struggle, but it can lead to renewed life and purpose. That is a message people need to hear from their pastoral leaders, particularly from ones who can also testify to having personally "been there" themselves.

Peer Consultation

Quotations from parish staff persons in the guide come from three focus groups conducted in August 2012 at the Archdiocese of Chicago, and from responses to a survey of parish staff members who experienced a pastor transition during 2011 or 2012. Their valuable insights and contributions inform the text, particularly the strategies and conversation questions.

Some questions asked of parish staff were:

"How did the staff recognize the contributions of the current pastor before departure?" Sample response:

"We planned a Mass of Gratitude and party for the
parish. The planning was an essential tool as we dealt
with the emotions surrounding his leaving."

**"What would you like to say about your pastor tran-
sition experience?"** Sample response: "Overall, I'd say
it has been a fairly smooth transition. There are many
issues to be addressed in the parish at the moment,
and time is definitely needed to help sort this out. On
the other hand, trust is needed from the new pastor in
order to help staff members continue to do their jobs
well and effectively in order for the best collaborative
efforts to evolve."

Responses like these remind us that transition evokes a
wide array of emotions and requires adjustment from everyone
involved. There are no shortcuts. The process must work at its
own pace. As parishioners and staff come to accept the new
pastor, and he in turn comes to understand their history and
current situation, mutual trust begins to grow and openness to
change increases.

The reality is that staff, parishioners, and pastors *expect*
change. All would be naïve to think otherwise. Everyone in
the faith community, from their place in the system, needs to
discover how the change can evoke vitality and grow parish
mission. They will be well served by tapping into one another's
wisdom through faith-, hope-, and love-oriented conversations and consultations with those who have traveled similar
pathways.

Notes

1. Pope Benedict XVI, "Meeting With Clergy," *Origins*, 37, no. 11
(August 16, 2007), 190.

The Spiritual Dimensions of Pastor Transition

Pastor transitions are paschal mystery experiences. The community of faith is extended an invitation to walk the road with the disciples—and one another—to discover God's presence in and through the experience. It is a time of reflection, prayer, and celebration.

Like the disciples on the road to Emmaus, who were struggling to make sense of "all that had happened," you too may find it difficult to see, to understand, and to trust in the midst of a pastor transition. The surprising paradox is that precisely in this confusion and chaos, when you do the simple acts of recalling your story, sharing hospitality, and breaking bread together, you rekindle your hearts.

The Emmaus story is a "round trip" journey that begins with discouragement, grief, and confusion, and ends with hearts burning, a new vision, and a renewed urgency to share the Good News (Luke 24:13-35). In *Dining in the Kingdom of God*, Eugene LaVerdiere places this story in context: the disciples were meant to be prophetic teachers; they were to remind the community of what Jesus said and did; and they were to help the community understand events that were being fulfilled in their midst. Yet, before they could take up that role, they needed to be reminded of all that had taken place and its meaning.[1] Having experienced the journey, when the disciples returned to the community, they and the community were at a very different place:

- in their understanding of the meaning of events,

- in their recognition of their relationship with Christ and one another,

- in their renewed call to share the Good News with hearts burning.

The time of pastor transition is a time of grace. It offers the possibility of renewal, for each member of a parish staff and for the parish as a community. Parish employees must take time, personally, with one another, and with parishioner leaders to reflect on all that is taking place and to ponder its meaning. Several parish staff persons mentioned the sustaining power of reflection and prayer on their journey through a pastor transition:

"(I) prayed a lot. Personally, I prepared myself to be as open and accepting of the new pastor as possible."

"Prayer and the support of a spiritual director (helped me through the transition)."

"Having to be present (to others) to do my labor for Christ, I took a personal retreat, I prayed, and asked for prayers."

"(I) breathed a sigh of relief and prayed for the people of the parish that their new pastor would recognize what a special group of people they are."

While each person must tend to his or her own personal work, it is by no means a solitary journey. There is a community of faith that has gone before and gathers around with their wisdom and hope for the future. You are encouraged to walk the journey with your questions, listen to the stories of God's presence in new and unexpected places, and break bread with strangers. Come to the table and share the

They were all astounded and bewildered, and said to one another, "What does this mean?"   *(Acts 2:12)*

holy bread and wine of our shared lives through the word that will be broken open by a pastor transition at your parish.

Invited into the Space of Transition

As a central premise of the INSPIRE Project, pastoral teams came to understand their parishes as living, organic systems. The health and vitality of Catholic parishes rely on pastors and pastoral leaders. INSPIRE's research explored emerging best practices in collaborative pastoral leadership in parish life. Soon after the project launched, pastor transition surfaced as a critical challenge to ministers and parishioners alike. Project leaders learned that, particularly at points of leadership transition, opportunities for persons to do personal work needed complementary settings for supportive conversations, discernment, and planning. This guide serves the unique perspective of parish staff during pastor transition. Companion resources include a pastor guide and a guide for parishioner leaders. The three texts may be used to foster reflection and dialogue among all engaged in the transition.

A pastor transition is a liminal experience bringing everyone to a threshold, an in-between time, in which the leaving is not complete and the arrival has not quite occurred.[2] The complexity of the experience grows as we consider the dimensions of each of the actors in the sys-

> Do not fear: I am with you;
> do not be anxious:
> I am your God.
> I will strengthen you, I will
> help you,
> I will uphold you with my
> victorious right hand.
> *(Isa 41:10)*

tem: the pastor who is leaving, the employees of the parish, the parishioners, and the pastor who is arriving.

Imagine transitional space as a room with an entrance on each of the four sides. While everyone enters into the same space, each enters from a different doorway (and at different times) and each sees the room from a different point of view.

One may walk in to find a blank wall facing them. Another's entrance reveals windows with flowers on the sills. Yet another doorway opens to a colorful wall that invites imagination. The fourth portal displays plaques and historical paintings. Everyone arrives focused on different perspectives about threat and opportunity, and each person brings previous experiences of transition.

Points for Reflection and Conversation

Pastor transition invites you into sacred space. To engage that space personally in prayer and reflection, you will need to set aside time and grow the disciplines of discernment. You can forge new relationships with both pastors—the one who prepares to leave and the one who arrives. Some of this you will do privately, yet some will play out in public and in communal settings with parishioners. It will be helpful to gather as staff persons to engage questions like those below. It may also be helpful to gather at other times with pastor and/or with parishioner leaders. The reflection points draw from the wisdom of pastors, staff persons, and parishioners who found themselves in the sacred space of waiting, wondering, wandering, and carrying on. They testify to the value of exploring the dynamics and opportunities that emerge when pastors change. As a staff person during this extended period of ecclesial expectancy, you are called to holy work.

Questions for Individual Reflection

1. What were my initial feelings when I heard that the pastor was leaving?

2. How have I navigated past transitions? What have I learned about myself in these times? Is there something I want to do differently?

3. What moment on the Emmaus Road journey speaks to how I am experiencing this transition?

Questions for Group Reflection

1. What is the view of the "transition space" from a parishioner doorway? How has the parish dealt with past transitions?

2. What does this transition mean for our pastor who is leaving? What might be the view of the "transition space" as he enters into this time?

3. What are the unique perspectives of various staff persons (custodian, choir director, youth minister, receptionist, school principal, and so on) that can help expand our collective understanding of this transition?

4. What pledges might we consider making to one another during this time?

Notes

1. Eugene LaVerdiere, *Dining in the Kingdom of God* (Chicago: Liturgical Training Publications, 1994), 157.

2. "Liminal space" refers to the experience of standing at a threshold, a time of "in between" what is passing and what is coming to be. It invites reflection and proactive observation, and as we will see, anything but inaction. Another parish staff person observed: "I was a 'dry sponge.' I was ready and willing to get started. I also tried to observe the dynamics that other staff members used. It was very unique because our pastor was there for (several) years and no one on staff had any experience in pastor transition."

The Journey of Transition

To better negotiate the challenges of a pastor transition, it is helpful to understand some of the dimensions of transition and keep in mind that a change of pastors affects

- the pastor,

- the parish staff,

- the parishioners, particularly parishioner leaders.

It is important to clarify the difference between change and transition. Some researchers speak of change as a shift in the *external* situation. In that view, transition is the *internal reorientation* one goes through in response to external change. It's not change itself that we fear, but the transition—the necessary interior adjustment with its array of emotions and stages.

William Bridges, who wrote extensively about organizational and personal transition, inverted the conventional "beginning, middle, end" progression and posited instead an "end, middle, beginning" construct as outlined here:[1]

> **Ending:** The departure phase, saying goodbye, leave-taking, letting go of what was, a time for mourning loss, for blessing and giving thanks for what has been, but also for clearing away ground in which new life can be seeded and take root.[2]

Neutral Zone: The in-between phase when persons experience the liminality of needing to leave where one is but not yet being certain about where one is going. It is a middle ground but much more than a waiting time, however. Leaders can make this a period of productive creativity, exploration, testing, and preparation. Living and working in the neutral zone can foster exploration, innovation, discovery, and learning. Leaders can pilot and test new working arrangements and procedures. Because they are explorations, even failures have lower cost and can be understood as valuable learning.

The New Beginning: The reentry phase focuses on adjusting to new surroundings and making them "home" while embracing new relationships and re- sponsibilities. Everyone learns to fold in continuing performances with some new ones. Realities of the new beginning become clear. Leaders must assess the new ground and respond to its challenges in positive ways.[3]

In any community transition it is unlikely that the neat order of scenario with stages will play out perfectly and sequentially. There are two important reasons. First, though one of the stages may be foremost in our aware- ness, in some ways dynamics of the other two remain active. The "new beginning" of the new pastor's arrival, for instance, beckons most everyone's awareness that they no longer stand in the presence of the departed pastor, and the "ending" stage reasserts itself. The new pastor too is likely experiencing comparable realiza- tions: "This sure isn't the same parish anymore!"

Second, people in a community enter and pass through these stages at different times and at different speeds. It isn't uncommon for any of the parish leaders,

themselves finally perceiving the arrival of a new beginning, to come up against the challenges of parishioners
who are just beginning to grieve the loss of their beloved
pastor.

The Exodus story provides a helpful illustration of the three-
part scenario. Israel departed Egypt and left behind much of
its identity. The people entered the in-between place of desert
ground, and they were sorely tempted to return to the fleshpots
of Egypt. They longed for the familiarity and predictability
of their former lives. Finally they neared the Promised Land,
approaching with great trepidation. So they wandered in the
wilderness, their neutral zone. Only after two generations of
living together and learning some hard lessons about living as
a people faithful to their God did they finally enter and claim
their place in the new land.

External circumstances or interior dispositions can frustrate
a productive experience of the middle ground. If the pastor's
leaving is abrupt, there may not appear to be opportunity to
honor the ending. If the pastor's retirement has been on the
horizon for quite some time, most may be ready to move more
quickly to a new beginning with a new pastor. However, leaders
(especially the pastoral staff) need to be assertive about creating
observances of endings. Also when changes are abrupt and a
new pastor comes—as some do—overnight, it is also important
to declare a middle ground adjustment period. It is difficult to
remain in the liminal space long enough to be strengthened
because it lacks handholds like clear policies and routines. For
parishioners and for the pastoral team, however, it can be a
critical time for discovery and growth. A staff person spoke of
this challenging work at a focus group:

*"Liminal space can be joyous with expectation of something
new. I've been through two transitions. We had INSPIRE*

help us with the last transition. That made a big difference.
We concentrated on the impact of the transition on all of us.
With the previous pastor (transition) there was nothing like
that, and it took us a long time to get to know him, and we lost
a lot of staff people in the year that he came."

Staff persons must focus on retrieving a personal sense of balance. An extensive middle ground holds rich opportunities for spiritual tending and reflection. It is an important time to reconnect with one's call to ministry. With the help of a mentor or spiritual advisor, it is important to recall how and why one serves this particular faith community. Like the disciples walking the road to Emmaus, it is important as a parish staff to dialogue about perceptions concerning the coming change in pastors. Staff members can (and usually they must) grieve, while calling one another to explore

> Now that very day two of them were going to a village seven miles from Jerusalem called Emmaus, and they were conversing about all the things that had occurred.
> *(Luke 24:13-14)*

the emerging possibilities inherent in a pastor transition. In safe spaces that honor confidentiality, a staff can sort out feelings of loss, unresolved concerns, and even glimmers of what the good might be that will surely arrive with such a significant change.

Mapping the Pastor Transition

Working with parishes in all stages of transition, INSPIRE consultants assisted pastoral leaders as they wrote personal and team continuing education plans to strengthen four competencies critical to healthy ministry:

- Ministerial skills,
- Appropriation of the Tradition,
- Personal and team integration,
- Spirituality.

> And it happened that while they were conversing and debating, Jesus himself drew near and walked with them, but their eyes were prevented from recognizing him.
>
> *(Luke 24:15-16)*

The project's pastoral teams that dealt with significant change issues, including pastor transition, discovered two kinds of invaluable assets: a personal executive coach and a clearness group. A coach or a clearness group engages a parish staff person with questions that foster clarity and self-awareness. Conversations occur at critical points throughout the transition. Typically, executive coaches bring training and credentials to the relationship.[4] Clearness groups follow a discernment practice developed in U.S. Quaker communities. A group forms when a person seeking assistance invites trusted colleagues and/or parishioners who bring a diversity of perspectives and thought. You can find a description of the process by Parker Palmer and resources at: http://www.courage renewal.org/parker/writings/clearness-committee.

From this learning "on the ground" and following William Bridges's three stages as a framework, pastoral possibilities emerge for parish teams to consider.[5] Because pastor and staff often precede everyone else into the space of transition, they are in unique positions to serve others in the transition process. Focusing their work, both personally and as a team, enhances their ability to invite parishioners as companions on the journey of transition.

Tending to the transition is ideally both a personal and a team engagement. To grow a vibrant community of faith, the following dimensions serve to help everyone in mapping out the journey of transition:

- Personal preparation,
- Pastoral or parish staff exploration,
- Involving parishioner leaders,
- Engaging the wider parish community.

It is important to remember that, as with any trip, mapping the journey (while necessary and helpful) is limited in its ability to predict the lived experience. The mystery of the journey resides in the movement of the Spirit in and through the hearts of the faithful. Be prepared for unmapped detours and expect the possible appearance of a stranger on the road.

Points for Reflection and Conversation

Pastor transition invites you into a time of self-assessment and self-care, and simultaneously into a time for exercising collaboration with staff, with those you serve, and with parishioner leaders. As a staff member, parishioners look to you for cues of how the transition is going. If you are going to be available to parishioners as they deal with the transition, the first work is getting to a personal sense of balance and priorities. It is like the safety instructions given before each flight takes off: "If in the event that oxygen is needed, secure your own oxygen mask before assisting others."

Next, you need to strive for productive, healthy engagements with others. Your outgoing pastor himself may be available to you and the staff. Those with whom you minister, colleagues on staff in particular, can be critically effective reality testers, co-planners, and sources of affirmation. Don't overlook those parishioners or staff for whose ministries or assignments you are responsible. Wisdom is to be found throughout the faith community.

Questions for Individual Reflection

1. Because the work of transition requires significant energy, what will I put on hold or stop doing to free up energy and time?

2. What support, reminders, and encouragement do I need during this time?

3. Whom might I call upon to serve as mentor or coach or advisor?

4. Who relies on my leadership, and what can I offer them?

Questions for Group Reflection

1. How would we title this chapter of life for the parish?

2. Have any of us gone through previous transitions? What is our collective wisdom?

3. What do we ask of each other?

4. How shall we assist our pastor as he prepares to leave?

5. How could we prepare to receive, welcome, and initiate positive relationships with the arriving pastor?

Notes

1. William Bridges, *Managing Transitions: Making the Most of Change*, 3rd ed. (Cambridge, MA: Da Capo Lifelong Books, 2009), 3–10.

2. One parish staff person spoke of the challenge of saying goodbye: "It was a definite dying for me because of my relationship with the former pastor. We had carried each other through many, many things."

3. A pastoral associate faced the new beginning head on: "Since the (arriving) priest was from Africa, I sought advice from others who had experience with priests from other cultures. I also prayed a lot!"

4. An accessible resource to learn about executive coaching maybe found at http://www.coach22.com/discover-coaching/resources/leadershipcoachingchapter1.pdf This web site offers resources for Christian communities.

5. At a focus group a pastoral associate reported the effectiveness of shared discernment: "The (departing) pastor helped us to manage and prepare (for the transition)—figuring who might be available and who would be a good person for our parish. That process helped us a lot."

Endings Put Us on the Road

Endings begin as soon as a person hears the pastor is leaving and flow beyond the physical leave-taking. The work of this stage includes recalling stories, honoring what has been shared, seeking forgiveness and acceptance, and expressing gratitude.

Personal preparation is not a luxury during times of transition. It is vital for staff persons to gift themselves with time and support to nourish and center their body, mind, and spirit. Identifying and scheduling spiritual practices (journaling, spiritual direction, physical activity in nature, a retreat) can positively influence how one experiences the transition.

Taking time to review personal continuing education plans invites a truly valuable exploration. Simply committing to a reading or a learning opportunity inevitably encourages new thinking. Such activities raise possibilities that can allay fears and challenge comfortable busy work that avoids transitional realities. Inviting a trusted mentor to be a supportive companion can encourage dialogue and reflection during a journey that offers both uncertainty and possibility.

Scouting as a learning team is an effective preparatory endeavor to explore concepts and patterns of pastor transitions.[1] Talking with other parish staffs that have traveled the road recently can surface what worked well for them. The learning team may choose to invite a speaker or include common readings as part of their agenda. Such resources create a context for raising questions, concerns, and hopes among the staff, and stimulate dialogue. Inviting a parish consultant to walk with the learning team during the transition provides support in creating safe conversational space. A pair of "outside eyes" can help the team surface and understand hidden dynamics and identify new resources. A consultant can ensure that everyone affected by the transition is included in the process.

Involving parishioner leaders invites key parish members into critically important dialogue and reflection. People learn how this challenging transition can actually empower the parish mission and expand what may be a limited vision. Encouraging parish committees to participate in the planning of parish events that prepare the parish to say good-bye to the pastor strengthens ownership and engagement as a community of faith.

When pastor transitions do not include the community, people often experience the transition as "victims," as something done to them. Without voice and engagement of those who are known as councilors, organizers, and faithful parish workers, rumors usually run rampant, hurt feelings are isolated and unshared, and people often distance themselves physically or emotionally. When a parish staff encourages parishioner leaders to include transition planning in their agendas, the learning community grows. They are empowered to join in naming:

- what the transition means for the parish community,
- ways the parish can share its story and offer gratitude for the pastor's gifts and service to the community,
- events and persons who can join in the welcoming of the new pastor.

Engaging the wider parish honors relationships that have been built over time, encourages the community to recall shared sacred moments in people's lives, and celebrates the gifts given and received. To prepare for the pastor's leaving, it is important for the community to have multiple opportunities:

- to tell their stories,

- to recognize the times of struggle,

- to celebrate with thanksgiving.

The parish staff, often the organizers and weavers of parish life, take up an important mission during this time. The pastor may be hesitant to speak of his leaving, or he may not want to create a "big fuss" at his departure. The staff is in a key position to foster authentic ways the community can ritualize and celebrate their journey with the pastor who is leaving. The parish calendar is a good starting focus. Consult it to identify parish traditions and life moments through which parishioners may be invited to design and plan milestone events. Parishioners can see that announcements get communicated properly to ensure wide participation.

> See, I am doing something new!
> Now it springs forth, do you not perceive it?
> (Isa 43:19a)

This is a time when the parish can look back and name critical moments while in the pastor's care. Recalling how such events effected life and renewal helps people join in the work of letting go. Moreover, they can begin to recognize God's providence in sending them leaders and ministers who believe in them and count on them.

Points for Reflection and Conversation

As a staff member you may personally have mixed feelings. If you have developed a close working relationship with the pastor, this may be a difficult time for you. It may be hard to think about saying farewell, let alone welcoming an unknown pastor. Parish staff stated that they often find themselves "in the middle" between parishioners and the pastor.[2] During times of transition this feeling intensifies and can lead to staff feeling alone and concerned that parishioners are feeling abandoned. It is especially challenging for parish employees if they have been informed of the pastor's leaving, but the move has not been publicly announced to the parish.[3] Parish staff stated that there is a tendency to shift into focusing on "just doing my work" and not dealing with the emotions and uncertainty that are the fertile elements of transition times. The promise of this rich potential encourages parish staff members to not "skip" this vital dimension of their journey.

Questions for Individual Reflection

1. What would be a meaningful way for me to express my personal gratitude to the pastor and to honor the relationship that has been built through our shared ministry?

2. What resources and support do I need during this time? Who are the people who can be honest and encourage me to name and clarify what I am experiencing?

Questions for Group Reflection

1. How will the staff recognize the contributions that have been made during the tenure of the departing pastor?

> 2. How will announcements and information regarding the pastor transition be shared with the parish?
>
> 3. What ritual celebration would honor the pastor's ministry that he has shared with the parish?

Notes

1. A staff person described the value of scouting as a learning team in preparing for the transition: "Starting the INSPIRE Project we knew within two years we would be going through a pastor change. We used INSPIRE resources to work with both the staff and with parishioners. Having gone through this for two years we were well-prepared."

2. A focus group comment from one parish staff person expressed this reality: "I see myself as part of the process. I'm right in the middle trying to keep everyone together. There are (also) things I need to work on personally."

3. A staff member describes this experience: "It was quite difficult. People would ask me direct questions which I was not at liberty to answer. I felt I was not being honest with the people. They wanted explanations of Father's 'angry' behavior which I could not share."

Along the Road, Somewhere in the Middle

The middle ground on the journey of transition is a fertile time, but it can be uncomfortable. Anxiety may rise and motivation fall. Your pastor has yet to leave, but both you and he look ahead with increasing anticipation and growing urgency. Meanwhile, the next pastor is arriving. Later on, even the time of the new pastor's arrival is an extension of the middle ground. For you and him and the rest of the staff, and for the parishioners, it is a time of learning and adjustment. He is still a stranger to the community, and the community is mostly a group of strangers to him. For everyone, though, it is a time for growth. It is important to keep journey language and images alive. People's resistance along any part of the middle ground often indicates that "catch up" time is in order. It can be helpful when leaders walk slowly. The question for the parish is, "How can we come out of this transition with a deeper understanding and even a stronger relationship with God and one another than before it all began?"

How the transition is recognized in community radically determines how the liminal time is experienced by all involved: a parish secretary conveys this recognition as s/he answers the phone; the liturgical minister weaves this recognition into the planning of rituals; the parish school teacher reflects it when interacting with students and families. Offering hospitality to the "strangeness" of this time creates the possibility for the community to recognize God's presence in the sharing of the story and the breaking of the bread.

Personal preparation at this time is as basic as remembering to breathe, grieve, and give thanks. Savor the moments—both the informal, spontaneous times and the ritual celebrations with the departing pastor. It is important to embrace losses and setbacks as entry points for new ways of imagining one's ministry.[1] Pastoral change veterans advise: explore small ways to invite new energy into the daily routine; transform a ministry task by doing it in a new way; take time to reconnect with an energetic parishioner; invite a friend not associated with the parish to lunch, a movie, or the theater; clean out or rearrange a portion of your office space.

Scouting and learning focuses on simplicity and recognizing meaning in daily parish life moments. As the moving day draws near it can become challenging for staff and parish leaders to make decisions. The unknown future (what parish life will be like with the arriving pastor) begins to fill the space of committee meetings and while some projects may be coming to completion, other plans may be put on hold. It is important to nurture a climate of welcome, safety, and learning among the staff. Effective strategies include: clearing schedules as much as possible; convening routine meetings and consultations in a new space; praying together as a staff; some new routine, for instance, an afternoon tea time. When staff persons resolve to simply be present to one another, together they can breathe their way into the holy space where they can receive and welcome their new pastor.[2]

Ministerial staff persons can lead the way by making use of symbols and small rituals to evoke stability and meaning during this time. Table displays in a foyer or reception area might include photographs and sacramental symbols such as oils, stole, cross, Scripture. Staffs may express gratitude and thanksgiving by blessing the departing pastor and inviting his blessing on the staff. Blessings can happen privately, for instance at the end of a staff meeting, or publicly at a parish reception, celebration, or liturgy.

Involving parishioner leaders invites them to consider what has come to completion in the life of the parish and what is waiting to be born. It is not a time of establishing new rules and policies, but rather a unique space in the transition process to ponder, wonder, and explore new possibilities. Creating ways to re-center the parish in a community mission and vision can provide a common orientation along the middle ground roadway.

A challenging but dynamic possibility is for the learning team to discern together current issues in the parish that need to be addressed and then to ask the questions such as:

- What issues might best be addressed by the outgoing pastor?

- What issues ought to wait for the arriving pastor?

- Are there any actions that could be taken jointly by the two pastors, such as the planning of a departure/arrival liturgical celebration?

Engaging the parish can create a sense of "advent" expectation for what is about to be birthed in the community. Parish staff persons provide pastoral care during the transition by listening to parishioners' anxieties, fears, and hopes. They are called to listen, listen, and listen again as parishioners experience various stages of the journey at any one time. Staff can encourage parishioners to name their feelings and to recognize the multitude of emotions that accompany change.[3] Forgiveness and reconciliation also are important tending elements for leaving that which has been and bringing about healing and closure.

While resistance is a common dynamic among parishioners, some may want to rush ahead to establish a new "order" in the parish. They may want to preempt the sometimes tedious or disruptive exploration that characterizes middle ground learning. Valuing the in-between space offers the most fertility and possibility

> Then they said to each other, "Were not our hearts burning [within us] while he spoke to us on the way and opened the scriptures to us?" *(Luke 24:32)*

for strength in the future. Movement along the liturgical seasons introduces opportunities to help the parish engage and remain in the productive middle time of pastor transition. Incorporating the liturgical seasons into the lived experiences of the transition invites the parish into prayer and reflection. Good prayer experiences spur parishioners' imaginations to cultivate positive scenarios of the future with the new pastor.

Points for Reflection and Conversation

It is vital for you to recognize the energy it takes to be present to both the pastor, who is leaving, and the parishioners. It is usually not a time for accomplishing major tasks. During the middle ground period, some days don't seem all that productive. You may find yourself going home at the end of the day wondering, "What have I done all day? I couldn't move the project forward because I need to wait for the new pastor's support." Remember that keeping vigil is one of the most exhausting and holy acts we can do for ourselves and for one another.

Jesus' promise to bring fire to the earth is offered on the road to Emmaus as "slow hearts to believe" become hearts burning within us.[4] The paschal mystery is not over at any one Easter. It stretches before us into the rest of our lives. As disciples, precisely because we once chose to engage the Stranger, life and ministry will never be the same. The good news, alive in us, propels us to minister to and with the community anew.

Questions for Individual Reflection

1. What has been my experience of keeping vigil, when calendars and plans are of little assistance?

2. How am I caring for my body, emotions, and spirit during experiences of high energy but low productivity?

3. What spiritual practices (journaling, spiritual direction, silent meditation, prayer circle, walks in nature, and so on) encourage the emergence of questions and help me keep my balance?

4. In what ways can I create the opportunity for making small choices to reclaim a sense of control for myself and others?

Questions for Group Reflection

1. How will staff ensure a listening presence to parishioners?

2. What would reassure and engage parishioners in the pastor transition experience?

3. What are ways that parish staff can invite parishioners to enter into the mystery of this space rather than rushing through to fill a void?

4. Are there speakers or programs that might help parishioners understand the issues and potential of pastoral transition (such as pastors or staff persons who recently experienced a successful transition)?

Notes

1. A parish staff focus group participant described the personal experience of this middle place on the road: "I think what I experienced was just grief. We lost a very popular pastor. To recognize that and to know that everybody is grieving, that's hard and very draining. Then you have to learn someone new and begin a new relationship with someone who is your boss. It is part of the reimagining of everything along with letting go."

2. At a focus group one staff person reflected: "There is a beauty in it. I try to accept it, though it is difficult in the moment. I try to put pieces together. The waiting for what is going to happen. There are changes that are hard and some that are good. You know it is going to happen, like the sunset. So, grab that moment because it is important."

3. At one of the focus groups a staff person spoke of focusing on the work of this phase of transition: "I need to give people hope and help them to find their voice."

4. Luke 12:49-50; 24:25-32.

Arrival at the Beginning

A new beginning involves new understandings, new attitudes and new identities. It reinforces that the ending is real and that in returning to a new beginning all are changed. There is no "going back to the way things used to be." Allowing time for a new beginning to take root strengthens the possibility that the parish can begin to recognize an understanding of itself in a new way.

Jesus recalled the story for the disciples on the road to Emmaus. The two disciples might be stand-ins for a parish that realizes its new beginning. The community once again claims a transformed identity and mission as a people of God. The anxieties, conversations, planning, and envisioning of past weeks and months re-centered the community. They are coming to new understandings of their values and mission as Church. The Emmaus story reminds the faithful what sustains them as a community. When they gather to worship as the people of God, they give everything over to God. They belong to God, and they belong to the Church neither because of the personality or particular charisms of a priest, nor because of their own efforts at controlling and ordering.[1]

When the liminal space is glossed over (pushing the pause button only long enough for the departing pastor to move out one day and the arriving pastor to move in the next) *everyone* can begin to feel like an outsider with no voice and no choice. A pastor transition is sacred work for the community, staff, and the new pastor. As they settle in with one another, they will name and claim who they are and why they break bread together.

William Bridges stressed the significance of the middle ground work for ensuring and maximizing the possibility of a productive new beginning. It is important for parish staff and parishioners to voice the questions that emerge during the transition. While it is too soon for answers, the invitation to raise the questions enhances the ability of the community to work together to begin to create responses to these concerns. A solid ground of reassurance is created when parishioners with the staff and arriving pastor have the opportunity to:

- tell their stories as a faithful community,
- recall their founding spirit and values,
- claim what makes them a unique community of faith,
- identify common vision and hopes for the future.

Personal preparation continues to be critical, as the new beginning reemphasizes the reality of the losses that came with the ending. There may be new pastoral responsibilities and new identities for each person on the parish staff. That requires time for adjustment. While the crafting of new job descriptions, revised policies and procedures are common at this stage, personal, internal reordering is really Job One. Growing and nurturing those disciplines of reflection, begun early in the transition, are truly important commitments now. Staff persons from Chicago observe that it's an appropriate time for some of the more challenging questions:

- For what that will never be quite the same again will I mourn and give thanks?
- What needs to be acknowledged as painful that I will give to God as an offering?
- Will I allow the Spirit to breathe new life into me, to become who I am called to be now?
- Next year at this time, what would really be life-giving for me and my ministry?

Scouting and learning prepares for new beginnings. As the arriving pastor faces the task of meeting many new people and adjusting to a different living and work environment, he begins to get a grasp on the various tasks and issues. He also needs to get to know his parish staff. Unspoken assumptions, a different leadership approach, and personality traits can create tension, avoidance, and defensive behavior among staff and with the new pastor. Staff persons are not in complete control here. They cannot demand personal and team meetings, but there are ways they can influence productive and positive encounters when they do occur.

Creating a simple way for the staff to welcome and bless the arriving pastor creates a positive tone for seeding healthy working relationships. Clear and honest communication, access to information, and clarity regarding decision-making processes become priorities as the parish staff and pastor move into building trust.[2] Orienting new staff who joined the team during the transition generates a welcoming atmosphere. New employees can begin to share their talents and gifts in ways that fit the culture and mission of their new parish. It is important to remind one another that transition happens much more slowly than change. Time is needed for hearts, minds, and spirits to "catch up" with the change, begin to discover meaning, and to develop mutual relationships.

Parish learning teams can find it helpful to invite a retreat leader to guide the staff in re-visioning their work for the coming year. This time "set aside" as a parish staff recognizes the year as a new beginning that offers the gift of exploration and discovery. A retreat experience can be a signal that this pastor and staff will routinely scan assets and opportunities that emerge in the months ahead.

Involving parishioner leaders through meetings of councils and committees is important during the new beginning. They may be invited to develop brief pastor orientations to their roles and work in progress. The reporting opens doors for the pastor's questions and indications of his pastoral interest. Parish staff can be a primary resource in introducing the arriving pastor to key parish leaders and parish routines.[3] They can also assure him that they can "have his back," as one staff told their new pastor. Parishes are rife with meetings and gatherings, and everyone wants the pastor with them. Most also have agendas to share. "It's like being under a funnel pouring out everyone's expectations and needs," said the same pastor. Staffs can help schedule manageable meetings with the pastor. As the new beginning moves into the initial months, it is helpful for council agendas to include intentional dialogue about discoveries that emerged throughout the transition. They should exercise caution about serving up long lists of decision items and agenda. The best new pastors avoid making big changes early on. They typically spend the entire first year getting to know their people and parish needs, and their main methods for learning are asking questions and observing.

Engaging the parish to provide a welcoming environment suggests multiple opportunities for parishioners to welcome the arriving pastor. While he needs to learn who they are, they need to learn who he is. At liturgies, school programs, youth gatherings, and so on, there can be receptions and small programs that introduce and welcome. These are critical moments for mutual recognition. One staff member at a focus group was adamant about helping the parish with the reality of transition:

> The fruit of the Spirit is love, joy, peace, patience, kindness, generosity, faithfulness, gentleness, self-control. Against such there is no law.
> *(Gal 5:22-23)*

"It would be nice if there were a workshop for the parish. People need to be reminded, 'You had Fr. _____ and these were his gifts. Now Fr. _____ is coming and here are his gifts. Value what you had and honor it so that you can look toward the new person and experience his gifts.' I think people need a reality check that the new pastor is not going to have the same gifts as the former pastor."

Points for Reflection and Conversation

During the early space of beginning anew, as you begin to look ahead, you may experience an amazing burst of personal creativity. The mystery of the liminal flows into this time. There can be a sense of permission that encourages your adopting new and different approaches. The freedom to claim this space as a time of exploration and settling in becomes a great gift that staff, lay leaders, and arriving pastors can give one another. Learning together, the community can generate new ministry offerings and collaborative practices. While these precious few months are temporary, when lived with intention and wonder, they offer potential for rich discovery.

The stories recalled in Easter season are good reminders of the shadows that may frighten us along the way. Doubt arose often in those early days. So, it is no surprise that reports of Jesus' repeated appearances included his offering of assurance, peace in the midst of the disciples' fear, anxiety, and uncertainty.

- The disciples invited the stranger in to dwell with them and discovered a fire in their hearts that energized them to immediately return to the community with hope (Luke 24:13-35).

- Jesus told his followers, exhausted after catching nothing, to try casting their net on the other side, the place where they were not expecting a response (John 21:1-14).

- And at breakfast on the beach, while resting and taking nourishment, Jesus challenged the disciples to follow him—to have the courage to use their gifts and minister to others in a new way (John 21:15-19).

Questions for Individual Reflection

1. Where are opportunities emerging to exercise creativity in ministry?

2. What can I do personally to welcome the new pastor?

Questions for Group Reflection

1. How will the parish ritualize the welcoming of our new pastor? How will staff provide support and resources and encourage their efforts?

2. What communication patterns within our parish staff provide strength for this time? What patterns are blocking us from establishing trust and developing productive working relationships?

3. If Jesus met our staff for breakfast on the beach, what would he say to us?

Notes

1. Margaret Wheatley speaks of joining in community that resists the urge to control everything. She quotes Erich Jantsch, "In life the issue is not control, but dynamic connectedness" and then goes on to say, "I want to act from that knowledge. I want to trust this universe so much that I give up playing God. I want to stop holding things together. I want to experience such security that the concept of 'allowing'—trusting that the appropriate forms will emerge—ceases to be scary. I want to surrender my fear of the universe and join with everyone I know in an organization that opens willingly to its environment, participating gracefully in the unfolding dance of order." See *Leadership and the New Science: Discovering Order in a Chaotic World* (San Francisco: Berrett-Koehler Publishers, 2006), 25.

2. Trust was named as a key factor for one staff person at a focus group: "Our new pastor had a great trust in the staff when he arrived. He told us we seem to be a vibrant parish and wanted to learn how we

do things. That he didn't have a need to come in and shake things up. He asked us to not compare him to anyone we had in the past and stated, 'I am just me.' The trust was reassuring because we had been a part of the community for many years. For many of the staff this was their home parish. It felt seamless even though he has gradually introduced changes."

3. A staff person at a focus group recalled this experience: "The new (pastor) came in with his suitcase knowing nothing and knowing no one. For the staff it was utter confusion. I felt my role was to be his ambassador and to introduce him to councils and committees."

Paradox for Parish Employees during Pastor Transitions

Psychologist Will Schutz identifies three basic needs for productive relationships.[1] These basic needs are also of fundamental importance in people's reaction to change:

- The need for *control* over one's environment/destiny,
- The need for *inclusion* in the process of change that is taking place,
- The need for *openness* and access to information.

It is a paradox that, precisely when they are feeling vulnerable regarding their positions at the parish during pastor transition, parish staffs are often stabilizing resources for parishioners. Questions regarding professional livelihood emerge. Will I still have a position at this parish? Will my responsibilities change as the arriving pastor brings a different leadership approach and skill set to the parish team? These questions are based in reality and need to be considered.

The INSPIRE project learned that parish staff who gathered together to reflect on these questions created an open environment that provided a "booster shot" for parish employees in two ways. First, the dialogue brought the shadow of uncertainty into the light of acknowledgment. Rather than silently lurking in the background, fears and anxieties became available for exploration. Second, occasions to share personal and professional concerns increased mutual understanding. It also made "counter-scenarios" possible, as people expressed their hopes and desires. As everyone considered possibilities for their future together, positive scenarios could grow, and discussions could turn to how to help them come about.

As the INSPIRE project worked with parish learning teams over a ten-year period, evaluations identified the importance of personal professional ministry development.

At present we see indistinctly, as in a mirror, but then face to face. At present I know partially; then I shall know fully, as I am fully known.
(1 Cor 13:12)

Strong, recurring commitments to learning and spiritual formation typified staffs that saw themselves as pastoral leadership teams. Parish employees were encouraged to seek out resources to strengthen their skills, regularly assess if they were working in areas of their passion, and to explore untapped possibilities for ministry in the world. Learning new skills or gaining new knowledge positively impacted a pastoral team's ability to navigate transitions.

Leadership change naturally creates openings for each person to reflect on her or his own path and explore where it might lead. As daunting or trite as it may sound, a healthy practice is the updating of one's resume

A staff person shared the importance of intentionally recognizing the potential a pastor transition offers: "I take (it as) an opportunity. I know it, but it is a good feeling to express it, to see how I put it together. Change is not always bad. (It is) challenging, but with faith (I) recognize that doors do open when others are closing. (I am) realizing how far I've come. I'm not being pulled by the negative energy."

and personal continuing education plan. Actually, such review and updating ought to be an annual practice. The process invites both recognition and discovery. It cultivates feelings of achievement, recognition of areas for growth, and sometimes it opens a longing for expanded horizons. A director of religious education reported taking this discipline to the next level. He actually identified new options for employment in his ministry field. The practice gave him the power to actively choose from some

A seasoned staff person affirmed the possibility the pastor transition provided as a professional minister: "It was an opportunity for me to announce my retirement. I have this year to walk with the new (pastor). But it is just a year. That has been helpful for me. This transition has been an opening for me."

attractive options. His choice to stay on affirmed for him and the parish that he was in a place "that I really wanted to be, rather than had to be." Reflection can result in:

• gaining clarity about the ministry one wants to do and identifying responsibilities one no longer wants,

• identifying opportunities to deepen one's skill sets, and so be challenged to seek new responsibilities,

• discovering that the life-giving option is to take on an entirely new path.

Staffing changes of some kind are common when pastors change. Avoidance is a tempting option. One may immerse oneself in work that distracts one's conscious attention to the dynamics of transition. Pulling away and not confronting the realities invites isolation and a sense of powerlessness. If and when changes happen, staff members who have prepared themselves can be proactive in taking on new responsibilities and developing positive new working relationships.

The possibility of growth and transformation during a time of pastor transition is reflected in a focus group response: "I discovered health and strength in an unhealthy system. I went through a process, with the help of the archdiocesan office, to express what needed to be addressed with others. Everyone was caught in the transition. When I was going through it, I never thought I would react like I did. It was painful. Yes, there were bad days. It has a lot to do with trust. I always knew there would be a reason why."

It is challenging work to speak with authenticity and generosity of spirit when staffing decisions are being made. Honest reflection, often supported by a coach or spiritual director, can make a great difference in emotional, spiritual, and physical health for parish ministers and those they serve.

Points for Reflection and Conversation

As you, your colleagues, and the pastor work to build trust, strive to achieve clear and honest communication, access to information, and clarity regarding decision-making processes. Your best communication skills are needed in staff conversations and collaborations. Make promises to provide feedback and to check unspoken assumptions. Agree to be ready for surprises. Just when it seems everything is running smoothly, some jarring glitch may arise. There is wisdom in the Church's Liturgy of the Hours during the Easter season. Each day the community prays aloud "Alleluia, Christ is risen" to remind us that regardless of how we are feeling, our faith *is* alive, Christ *is* risen. The "Easter season" of a pastor transition may take everyone a good fifty days to pray and to believe what they pray: "Yes, we are rising. Yes, there is new life emerging. Alleluia!"

Questions for Individual Reflection

1. In my ministry during the transition, do I find myself engaging or distancing myself from parishioners and other staff?

2. Where am I in the life cycle of my professional ministry? Am I:
    - still learning and discovering ways to use my gifts?
    - doing what I enjoy?
    - comfortable that my skills are a good fit with my responsibilities?
    - still energized by my work and where I am?
    - hungry for a new creative challenge?

3. Do I take time to reflect on and honor the good work I have done here?

> **Questions for Group Reflection**
> 1. What may be different these days in how the staff and parish leaders are functioning, communicating, collaborating, sharing faith?
>
> 2. What support or resources could assist the staff as a learning team during this time?
>
> 3. What gaps in parish life might there be? What could be going on that isn't yet?

> As he blessed them he parted from them and was taken up to heaven. They did him homage and then returned to Jerusalem with great joy, and they were continually in the temple praising God.
> *(Luke 24:51-53)*

The End Is the Beginning

When the sacred work of transition is a journey guided by faith, hope, and love, both persons and communities grow: in spiritual strength, in relationships, in common vision and mission. Transitions are times for risks well worth taking. Transition journeys are wandering, unpredictable, and very human.

Experience tells us that

- if we tend well to our endings, acknowledging losses and putting them into recollection of our Sacred Story,

and

- if we are willing to remain long enough in the strengthening "in-between" place, exploring the spaces created by the change—and somewhere along the road welcoming the Stranger, *then*

- the possibilities for beginnings are infinite—welcomed and engaged because of a Spirit-fueled burning in our hearts, sending us back into our lives, families, and communities to share Good News.

Notes

1. Will Schutz, *The Human Element: Productivity, Self-Esteem and the Bottom Line* (San Francisco: Jossey-Bass, 1994).

Strategies
for Effective Transition

Mapping Your Pastor Transition Journey

In the following pages, you will find a collection of recommendations from Chicago pastoral ministers, organized according to the three-stages framework of William Bridges. It is important, especially for staff and pastors, to remember that individuals cross through these stages at different times. Furthermore, pastor transitions occur in some communities over just a matter of days, while for others the process can extend over several months. Pick and choose the strategies that appear to apply best to your own needs and circumstances.

Endings begin as soon as a person hears the pastor is leaving. They flow beyond the physical leave-taking. The work of this stage is to recall stories, honor what has been, seek forgiveness, express gratitude, and make space for all that will be new: persons, relationships, practices, and ministries.

1. Personal Preparation

- Set aside time for spiritual practices that will nourish and center you (journaling, spiritual direction, physical activity in nature, retreat, and so on).

- Explore reading and learning opportunities that will renew you and encourage new thinking. (See page 54 for a short bibliography.)

- Savor the moments—both informal spontaneous moments and ritual celebrations with the departing pastor.

- Ask someone you trust to mentor or coach you through this transition.

2. Staff Scouting and Learning

- Identify your work as a member of the staff or parish transition team.
- Seek out and talk with other parish staffs about what worked well at their parish during a pastor change.
- Use this book or other writing on transition as staff reading. Set dates to discuss your readings.
- If you have a large staff, divide into reading teams with different readings assigned to cover a broader spectrum of thought. Each reading team can report their learning to the larger staff.
- Invite speakers to conduct workshops on transition.
- Invite a parish consultant to walk with the staff during the transition.

3. Involving Parish Leaders

- Involve parish pastoral council in dialogue about the transition.
- Recommend readings to council and other parish groups and committees. The third guide in this series is written for parishioners, especially those serving in a wide array of leadership roles.
- Create committees to participate in the planning of parish events that prepare for the pastor's departure.

4. Engaging the Parish

- Review the parish calendar and identify traditions, anniversaries, and opportunities in which parishioners can participate in the transition.

- Determine how announcements will be communicated throughout the transition experience.

- Establish and publicize a fact finder or hotline service people can use to separate facts from rumors.

- Look for ways to help everyone in the parish practice the work of letting go.

Middle Ground is fertile liminal time that is often uncomfortable. Normalizing the experience with reminders of journey language and images helps to name the reorientation that is taking place. The question for the parish is, "How can we come out of this waiting time better than we were before the transition began?"

1. Personal Preparation

- Don't be surprised by feelings of loss that you still must acknowledge: breathe, grieve, and give thanks.

- Prepare to welcome the arriving pastor.

- Embrace losses and setbacks as entry points for new ways of imagining your ministry.

- Clear as many tasks as possible from your calendar.

- Build some new practice into your daily routine.

- Transform a routine ministry task by doing it in a new way.

2. Staff Scouting and Learning

- Plan a simple, meaningful way for the staff to bless the departing pastor.

- Strengthen a climate of welcome, safety, and learning as a staff.

- Consider creating new spaces—schedules and places— for meetings and dialogue.

3. Involving Parish Leaders

- Identify current parish issues needing to be addressed.

- Discern with parish leaders and the current pastor what issues are best addressed by the outgoing pastor, what issues need to wait for the arriving pastor.

- Develop rituals and hospitality for welcoming the new pastor.

- Consider a Sunday liturgy with both pastors present. There can be gestures of commendation and the handing on of symbolic items that affirm the exchange: rectory keys, parish baptismal registry, financial books, vestments, and so on.

- Review the parish mission and vision, look for ways to re-ground the parish in the mission and vision during this stage of instability.

- Consider a survey of parish ministries with updated lists of persons active in them.

4. Engaging the Parish

- Look ahead on the parish calendar and consider how the seasonal cycle of the church year offers opportunities to invite parishioners into prayer, reflection, and visioning for the future with the new pastor.

- "Listen, listen, listen!"

A New Beginning involves new understandings, new attitudes, and eventually new rules and routines. A well-tended new beginning takes root and strengthens the mission of the parish.

1. Personal Preparation

- By now you are probably aware of losses and deficits, as well as new pastoral work and identity for each person on the parish staff. Personally enter into a lenten reflection on your journey:

- For what that will never be quite the same again shall I give thanks and mourn?

- What needs to be acknowledged as painful and taken to the tomb, then given to God as oblation (as offering)?

- Will I allow the Spirit to breathe new life into me, to become who I am called to be now?

• Allow yourself to name that old feeling of loss: the new pastor's arrival confirms that indeed you have parted ways with your former pastor.

• Pray for your new pastor, including petitions of thanksgiving.

• Keep your spiritual life alive.

• See that your family knows about changes in your daily or weekly routine that will require their support and adjustment.

2. Staff Scouting and Learning

• Seek out opportunities to welcome the new pastor, to introduce him to staff persons and parishioners with whom you work.

• Create a simple way for the staff to welcome and bless the arriving pastor.

• As a staff, prepare a walking tour orientation to the parish.

• Identify times to review with the pastor the work that you do, especially your job description and calendar items for programs and activities.

• Give special attention to new staff who have joined the team during the transition.

- Invite a retreat leader to guide the staff in sharing prayer and reflection.

- About three months into becoming a new pastoral team, reserve time to scan assets and opportunities that are emerging.

3. Involving Parish Leaders

- Encourage councils and committees to create brief pastor orientations of their mission, goals, current responsibilities, and hopes for the future.

- With the pastor, work to update parish policies and to craft new policies that should be taken to the parish pastoral council for advisement.

4. Engaging the Parish

- Provide multiple opportunities for parishioners to welcome and create hospitality for the new pastor.

- Prepare bulletin articles, stories, and interviews for insertion during the first three months.

- If the new pastor arrives midyear, remember that some parishioners will only be settling back into parish involvement toward summer's end.

Tapping into the Gift of Symbols

Ritual and symbols are central for Catholics in expressing experiences that run deeper than words alone convey. At the Chicago staff focus group sessions on pastoral transitions, participants brought and reflected on symbols linked to their experiences. The stories they shared elicited rich insight and conversation. Inviting symbols to deepen communal reflection is a helpful tool, especially in times when the stakes include spiritual and emotional wellness.

Consider scheduling time on the staff agenda for reflection using rituals you develop that are relevant to the context of your parish. Use symbols that make sense to you. Do this at each stage of the transition: ending, middle ground, and a new beginning. Some ideas to build around are:

- Schedule gatherings and read a Scripture passage or poem that reflects the experience of individuals and the group.

- Use sacramental symbols of baptism, confirmation, and Eucharist. Have present a Bible and other explicitly religious symbols such as a cross, prayer card, rosary, crucifix, stole, or statue that are significant to the spiritual life of the parish. Invite volunteers and staff to bring in small items that are significant to them.

- Ask persons to share their thoughts and feelings about a particular symbol, and how it speaks to where they are currently in the transition process.

- Invite the group into silence, holding the current experiences and time together as sacred.

- Close with prayer and a blessing.

A Simple Staff Blessing of Farewell

During the tenure of a pastor, the staff and pastor weather many storms together. They learn from each other as they grow in their professional ministry. When acknowledging the end of their working relationship, the staff may extend their blessing to the pastor. Following are ideas just to get you started.

- As a staff project, build a blessing ritual. Compose a simple prayer, create a gathering area, add gestures.

- Create a special display that includes some symbols from home that the staff connects with the departing pastor.

- Invite each staff member to prepare a short blessing or a farewell note on a note card. Give the note cards to the pastor as remembrances of blessing and encouragement and suggest that he keep them accessible during the beginning days of his new assignment. These notes could also be compiled in a scrapbook.

A Simple Staff Welcome

While individuals welcome the arriving pastor in their personal style, it is helpful for the staff to welcome the new pastor as a team to recognize the beginning of their collegial working relationship.

- Build a welcome blessing ritual. Ask each staff member to bring a small item as a gift for the new pastor. Items should be simple, not costly, and may include household items.

- Share food, for instance at a luncheon, to enhance the welcome.

- Build in time for the pastor's blessing of the staff.

Ten Strategies for Staff during Transitions

1. Maintain open communication that creates a mutual exchange of information.

2. Assume that abundant resources for change and growth are already present in the community.

3. Strengthen relationships through mutual participation, respect, and encouragement. Look for opportunities to have contact with others. Distancing yourself can send signals of abandonment.

4. Empower yourself and make it possible for others in the community to be agents for change when necessary. Find ways that people can contribute.

5. Low energy is a hallmark of transitions. Lowering expectations of yourself and others recognizes the intensity of this work. Listen to your body and honor its need for rest and renewal.

6. Resist the urge to rush out of the middle ground. Look for ways to explore creative opportunities as they emerge. This offers potential for renewal in your ministry.

7. As a staff, model open communication and mutual trust. Parishioners will be watching.

8. Survey, recognize, and name how the pastor transition is affecting individuals and the entire community. Limit your urges to rescue, and give people space and time to make adjustments.

9. At the end of staff meetings, ask the question: Is there anything we didn't talk about today that needs to be discussed?

10. Pray alone and together. While the tasks of the transition can overwhelm you and sap energy, your work in the parish must be deeply rooted in the Church's rich traditions and theology of call and response, hospitality, healing, thanksgiving, and reception.

Five Ways to Be Present to the Parish Community in Transition

1. **Name the change**: Learn to describe the change succinctly and why it is happening. Craft your one-minute story about the change. Make it honest, open, hopeful. Invite parishioners to surface their own questions. Resist the urges either to dismiss anxieties or to rush in and fix emerging issues. Claim and celebrate new learning and discoveries.

2. **Create ritual:** Take steps to help people respectfully let go of the past and walk into the future. Use symbols that are

meaningful to the parish. Rituals can express the vitality and belonging we wish for the community.

3. **Sit with uncertainty:** Recognize that ambiguity is natural during transitions. Create space for experimentation, discoveries, and failures. Model for others a spirituality of walking by faith into the unknown.

4. **Communicate:** Listen and validate parishioners' questions. Be clear and firm when it is premature for answers. Encourage that particular concerns be directly communicated to an appropriate person, council, or committee.

5. **Be:** Take care of your own spirituality and health so that you have energy to be present to others. Parishioners draw assurance from a person whom they perceive as spiritually grounded.

Five Ways to Mess Up a Transition

1. Don't engage the larger community in the transition. Presume they have no need to know what is happening.

2. Assume that your position at the parish is in jeopardy.

3. Compare the new pastor with the previous pastor in conversations with parishioners and at staff meetings.

4. Continue to consult with the pastor once he has left or retired.

5. Establish a defensive stance, stop communicating, hunker down in your "silo" of ministry.

Five Commitments to the "Old" Pastor

1. You will honor his contributions to the parish.

2. You will express gratitude for guidance and learning through your professional working relationship.

3. You will never speak negatively of his ministry or draw comparisons to the good new things the new pastor is doing.

4. You will not share with him parishioners' concerns regarding the new pastor.

5. You will hold him in prayer as he transitions to his next assignment.

Five Commitments to the "New" Pastor

1. You will allow him time to get settled and "arrive" at the parish. Recognize that while the new pastor is physically at the parish, his head and heart may take some time to make the transition.

2. You will communicate openly, inviting his ideas and questions.

3. You will not compare him to other pastors but encourage him to be himself and to work out of his giftedness.

4. You will support him in taking time for himself and respect his days off.

5. You will hold him in prayer daily and seek his prayer for you.

Ten Personal Reflection Questions for Staff during a Pastor Transition

These ten questions are not presented as a check-off list, nor are they rigidly sequential. Work with them slowly over lengthy periods of time. They are written to provoke other questions.

1. What do I *value*? How is the ministry that I do enabling me to uphold these values?

2. What do I *want to accomplish* in this ministry? Is this happening or can it happen?

3. What do I *hold as true* for myself and for my work? What are my convictions? In whom or what do I believe? What do I believe I can do or be?

4. What *motivates* me? What energizes me in ministry? What lifts my spirit?

5. What am I *good at*? What are my skills?

6. What kind of *work environment* do I need?

7. What is my *body* telling me? Where am I physically with myself and with others? Where are my tension points?

> For God is the one who, for his good purpose, works in you both to desire and to work. *(Phil 2:13)*

8. Where is my *giftedness*? Where am I transfigured? Where do I light up? What is my "heart" gift?

9. What do I want my family to know?

10. *What do I really want?*

Bibliography

Books

Bridges, William. *Managing Transitions: Making the Most of Change*, 3rd ed. (Cambridge: Da Capo Press, 2009).

Hammond, Sue Annis. *The Thin Book of Appreciative Inquiry*. 2nd ed. (Bend, OR: Thin Book, 1996).

Hammond, Sue Annis and Andrea B. Mayfield. *The Thin Book of Naming Elephants* (Bend, OR: Thin Book, 2004).

Kelley, Robert. *The Power of Followership: How to Create Leaders People Want to Follow and Followers Who Lead Themselves* (New York: Doubleday, 1991).

LaVerdiere, Eugene. *Dining in the Kingdom of God: The Origins of the Eucharist According to Luke* (Chicago: Liturgy Training Publications, 1994).

Paddock, Susan Star. *Appreciative Inquiry in the Catholic Church* (Plano, TX: Thin Book, 2003).

Rost, Joseph C. *Leadership for the Twenty-First Century* (Westport, CT: Praeger, 1993).

Schutz, Will. *The Human Element: Productivity, Self-Esteem and the Bottom Line* (San Francisco: Jossey-Bass, 1994).

Sweetser, Thomas. *Keeping the Covenant: Taking Parish to the Next Level* (New York: Crossroad Publishing, 2007).

Wheatley, Margaret J. *Turning to One Another: Simple Conversations to Restore Hope to the Future* (San Francisco: Berrett-Koehler, 2002).

_____. *Finding Our Way: Leadership for Uncertain Times* (San Francisco: Berrett-Koehler, 2004).

_____. *Leadership and the New Science: Discovering Order in a Chaotic World* (San Francisco: Barrett-Koehler, 2006).

Whitehead, James and Evelyn Eaton Whitehead. *The Promise of Partnership: A Model for Collaborative Ministry* (Lincoln, NE: iUniverse.com, Inc., 2000).

Online resources

Archdiocese of Chicago Office for Lay Ecclesial Ministry, http://www
.archchicago.org/departments/lay_ecclesial_ministry/lay
_ministry.shtm

INSPIRE, www.inspireproject.org

Clearness Committee Model of the Center for Courage and Renewal, http://www.couragerenewal.org/parker/writings
/clearness-committee

A pdf format of a popular early William Bridges article,"Getting Them
Through the Wilderness: A Leader's Guide to Transition," that
illustrates leadership strategy in the Neutral Zone with reflection
about Moses in the Exodus, http://www.wmbridges.com/pdf
/getting-thru-wilderness-2006-v2.pdf

Article by Margaret Wheatley and Deborah Frieze that identifies
models of leadership in times of complex transitions: "It's Time
for the Heroes to Go Home," *Leader to Leader Journal,* Fall 2011.
http://www.hessel beininstitute.org/knowledgecenter/journal
.aspx?ArticleID=887